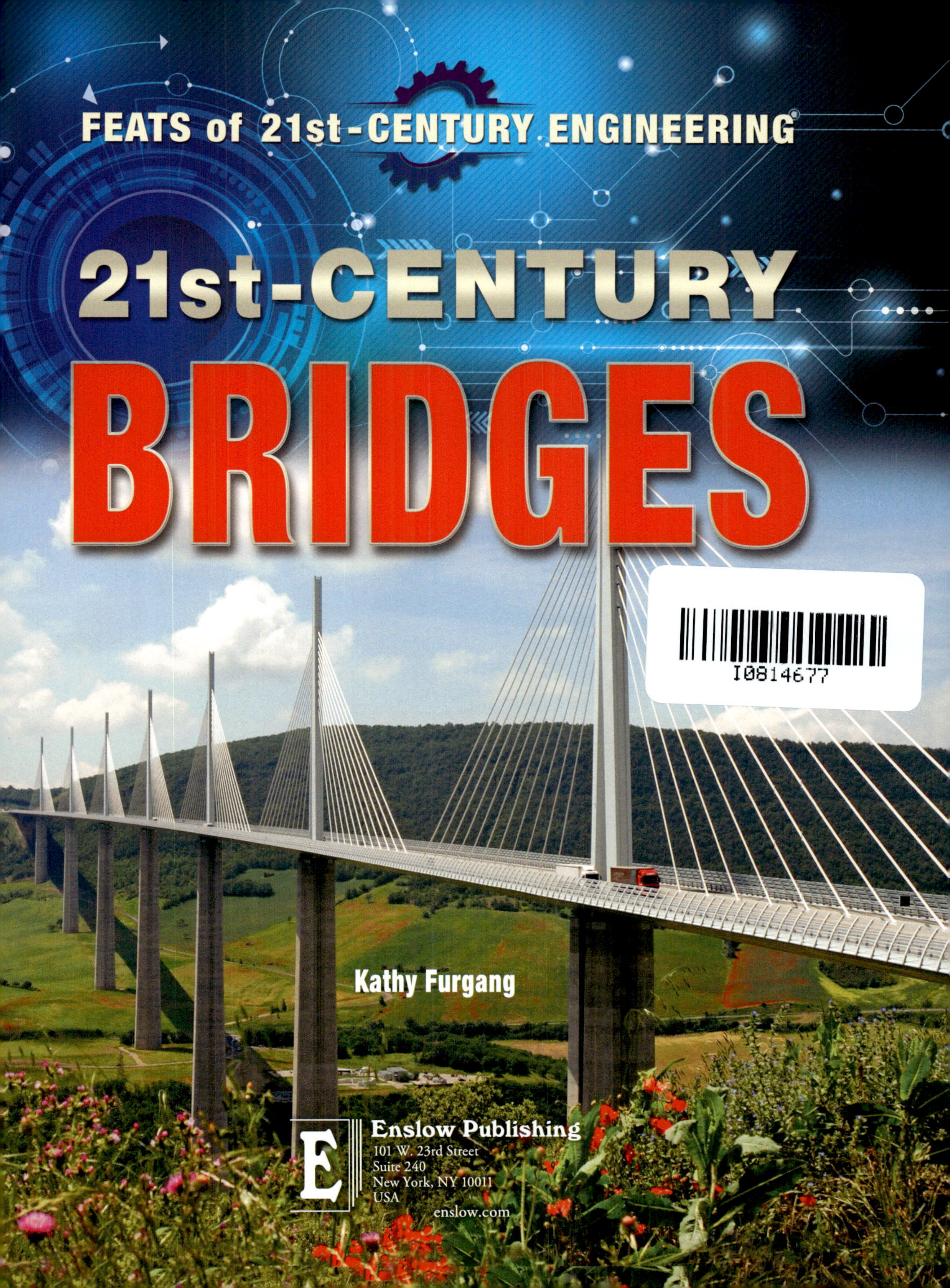

FEATS of 21st-CENTURY ENGINEERING

21st-CENTURY BRIDGES

Kathy Furgang

Enslow Publishing
101 W. 23rd Street
Suite 240
New York, NY 10011
USA
enslow.com

Published in 2019 by Enslow Publishing, LLC.
101 W. 23rd Street, Suite 240, New York, NY 10011

Library of Congress Cataloging-in-Publication Data

Names: Furgang, Kathy, author.
Title: 21st century bridges / Kathy Furgang.
Description: New York : Enslow Publishing, 2019. | Series: Feats of 21st century engineering | Includes bibliographical references and index. | Audience: Grades 3-6.
Identifiers: LCCN 2017048843| ISBN 9780766096943 (library bound) | ISBN 9780766096950 (pbk.)
Subjects: LCSH: Bridges—Juvenile literature.
Classification: LCC TG148 .F87 2018 | DDC 624.2—dc23
LC record available at https://lccn.loc.gov/2017048843

Printed in the United States of America

To Our Readers: We have done our best to make sure all website addresses in this book were active and appropriate when we went to press. However, the author and the publisher have no control over and assume no liability for the material available on those websites or on any websites they may link to. Any comments or suggestions can be sent by email to customerservice@enslow.com.

Photo Credits: Cover, p. 1 (technical drawing) pluie_r/Shutterstock.com; cover, p. 1 (bridge) Stanth/Shutterstock.com; p. 4 fiz_zero/Shutterstock.com; p. 8 Lanmas/Alamy Stock Photo; pp. 10–11 pisaphotography/Shutterstock.com; p. 13 somchaij/Shutterstock.com; p. 16 FocusTechnology/Alamy Stock Photo; pp. 18, 20 Bettmann/Getty Images; p. 24-25 © AP Images; p. 26 Jim Sugar/Corbis Historical/Getty Images; p. 28 steve007/Moment/Getty Images; p. 30 Michael Dwyer/Alamy Stock Photo; pp. 34-35 Iurii Buriak/Shutterstock.com; p. 37 ullstein bild/Getty Images; p. 38 KYTan/Shutterstock.com; pp. 40-41 Alexander Mazurkevich/Shutterstock.com; cover and interior pages (gear) plutonian/Shutterstock.com.

CONTENTS

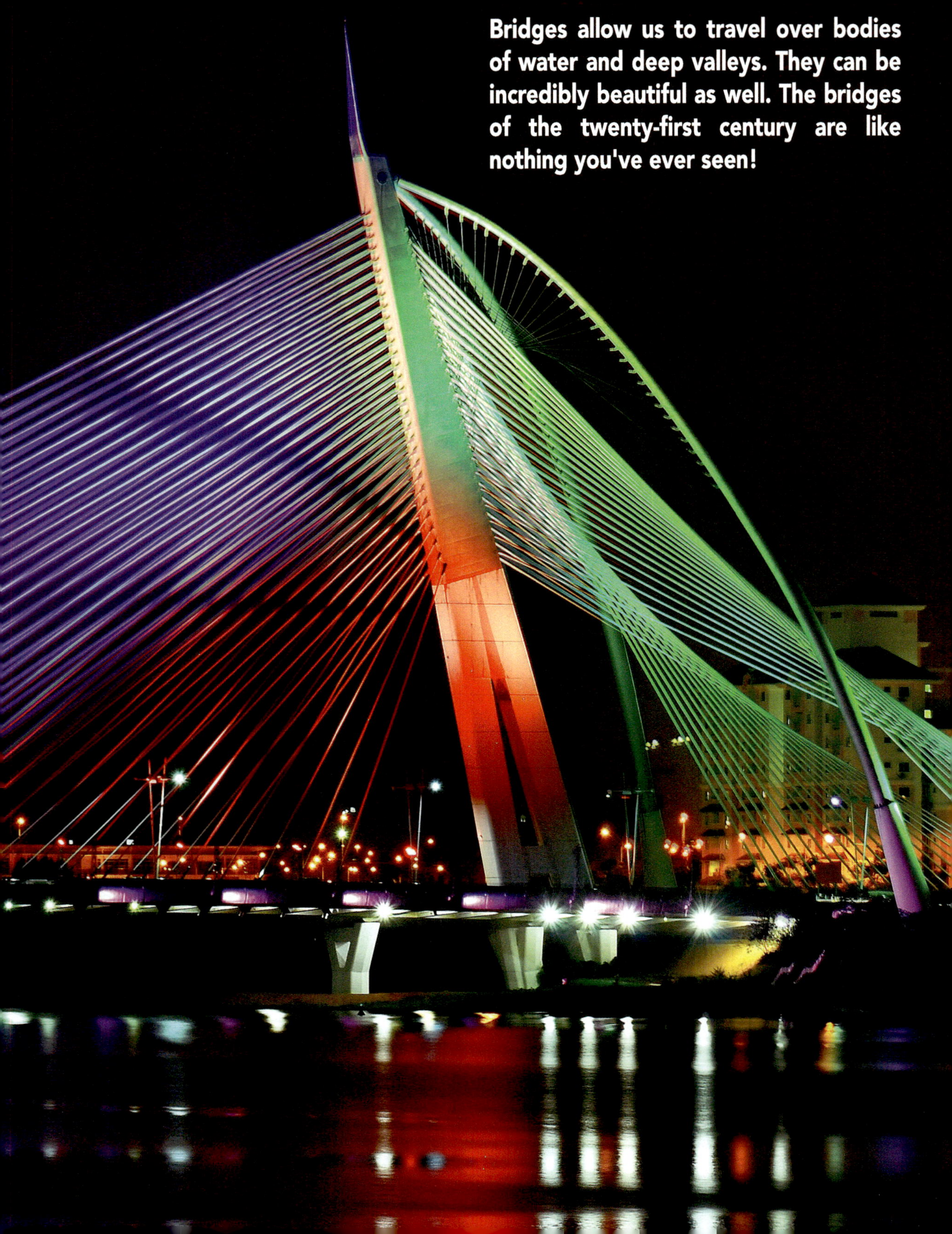

Bridges allow us to travel over bodies of water and deep valleys. They can be incredibly beautiful as well. The bridges of the twenty-first century are like nothing you've ever seen!

Introduction

Transportation is one of the greatest abilities that humans have. It might sound simple, but knowing how to get from one place to another involves a lot of knowledge. It's not just where to go that's important. It's how to get there. Throughout the history of mankind, humans have worked to figure out the best way to get from one place to another. Boats that travel over water are incredible inventions. Bridges that span water or valleys make travel much easier.

Bridges have been around since the earliest civilizations. Something as simple as a log placed over a stream can be considered a bridge. But a log bridge won't last long before it rots or breaks. It cannot carry very heavy loads. As time passed, people thought of new ways to improve bridges so they could hold more. They were constructed from stronger, more durable materials. They passed over greater distances. Instead of just passing over a stream, bridges could pass over wide rivers. A bridge could even connect mountains. Bridges cut down on travel time. They allowed people to explore other parts of the world much easier than before.

Today we have modern materials and technologies for building bridges. Bridges are stronger and more complex than ever before. Engineers are people who design, build, and maintain bridges and other structures. In the United States alone, there are more than 607,000 bridges. These bridges get people everywhere, from crossing over a simple highway to driving over a wide, raging river. Without bridges in the United States and other places around the world, travel would take much longer. Going around a river or a valley could add hours to a trip. Getting to certain places at all would not even be possible without bridges.

It takes civil engineers a lot of time, material, and skill to build and repair modern bridges. Today's bridges must be able to handle heavier traffic loads than ever before. The safety of the public is the most important thing when it comes to engineering. Modern engineers must make sure that bridges work well with any roads, canals, or dams they cross.

This book explores the future of bridges and how the design, construction, and materials must change to deal with the challenges that we will face in the future. Increased traffic and environmental issues are just a couple of the challenges that today's engineers face when they build bridges. The bridges built today must meet and succeed the challenges of our future.

Bridge-Building Basics

Mesopotamia, the world's oldest known civilization, thrived from 6000 to 530 BCE. Mesopotamia is part of today's Middle East region. This area is where the first bridges have been found. The simplest materials, such as wooden logs or stones, were used to connect one mass of land with another. Most bridges from thousands of years ago are no longer standing. However, some of them are still used today. One of the oldest bridges still standing today was made in this area of the world. The Caravan Bridge was built around 850 BCE over the Meles River in Izmir, Turkey. It is still standing today.

As time passed, the materials became stronger and more reliable. The Roman Empire was a more advanced civilization. It lasted from about 750 BCE to about 1450 CE. Instead of using dirt between stones, which washed away in the rain, the Romans discovered that ground-up volcanic rock made a good material for binding rocks together. This allowed for stronger and longer bridges. The techniques that these early engineers used were duplicated around the world. Bridges appeared in Europe and Asia. Some bridges were built to connect mountains, making foot travel easier.

This engraving of the Caravan Bridge in Izmir, Turkey, was made in 1890. The Caravan Bridge is one of the oldest known bridges still standing today.

In the Roman Empire, aqueducts were also built. An aqueduct is a bridge across a valley or other large gap of land. One end of the bridge is higher than the other, so it is slanted. A channel is made in the bridge so that water can flow from the top of the aqueduct to the bottom. This delivers water from a higher location to a lower location. Aqueducts were very helpful for the spread of the empire. Crops could be grown farther away from water sources because the water could be delivered to the crops. Most of these structures were made of stone.

Eventually, concrete and other building materials were used to construct bridges and make transportation easier. Once steel was produced on a large scale in the 1900s, bridge building became more of an engineering feat. Even though bridge-building techniques and materials changed over time, there are six basic types of bridges seen around the world: the beam, arch, truss, suspension, cable-stayed, and cantilever.

Beam Bridge

A beam bridge is the simplest type of bridge. It is simply a roadway sitting on top of supports. A short beam bridge may need supports only on the ends of the bridge. Other long bridges may have supports at set distances. These supports hold the weight of the traffic across the bridge. The weight that is added to the beam of the bridge is called the load. The more supports a beam bridge has underneath, the greater the load the bridge can hold.

For a simple bridge across a roadway or narrow waterway, a beam bridge can provide all the support needed. Many beam bridges have weight limits so that the load is not more than the bridge roadway

Building over Water

Many bridges are designed and built to span large bodies of water. It is important for the towers or abutments of a bridge to be sunk deep into the ground below a river. But how do construction crews work underneath the water to dig through rock and build bridges? Large airtight chambers called caissons are used. Workers are lowered slowly to the bottom of the body of water so that they do not suffer from the changes in air pressure. The caissons allow construction in places humans can't normally go or perform work.

and supports can handle. To support heavier loads, other bridge types are needed.

Arch Bridge

Builders have been constructing arch bridges for thousands of years. An arch bridge has a roadway that is supported by an arch underneath it. The semicircular shape underneath the bridge helps distribute

The Sydney Harbour Bridge in New South Wales, Australia, is an example of an arch bridge. The load of the bridge is distributed to the supports on either end.

the load to the two supports, called abutments, on either end. This allows the structure to spread the force of the load to the ends. When a force is applied to the top of the roadway as traffic passes over, the weight of that load is transferred to the stronger ends.

The greater the length of the bridge, the more arches are needed to spread out the load. The materials used are important, too. A stone arch bridge cannot support as much weight as a reinforced steel arch bridge. For example, some modern steel arch bridges can be over 1,000 feet (305 meters) long with the support of just a single arch. As builders plan and design bridges, they must be able to predict the loads they expect to pass over the bridge. This helps them choose the right materials and designs for the length the bridge will be.

Truss Bridge

A truss is a framework of connecting elements that gives extra support to a structure. Trusses are often made from a network of triangles. These give extra points of support to a square or rectangular structure. For example, if you make a cube out of popsicle sticks and place a large weight on top of it, the cube may break. But if you add extra popsicle sticks to connect one corner of the cube with ones diagonal from it, the structure becomes stronger. This extra support is called a truss. A structure with more trusses will be stronger.

In a similar way, a bridge will be strengthened by adding trusses to connect its supports. If engineers ever need to reinforce an existing bridge, trusses can be added to spread the load between the support points.

Suspension Bridge

Another type of bridge is a suspension bridge. With this type, the bridge's roadway is supported by a series of cables suspended between tall towers. The towers anchor the bridge and provide many points of support. As a load pushes down on the bridge's roadway, the cables transfer the weight to the towers. The towers provide grounding, and the load is transferred into the ground to support the bridge.

Suspension bridges provide a lot of support. They are interesting to look at, too. The Brooklyn Bridge in New York City and the Golden Gate Bridge in San Francisco, California, are examples of suspension bridges.

There are benefits to building suspension bridges. Getting support from cables means that fewer materials are needed for this type of bridge as opposed to other types.

The Golden Gate Bridge in San Francisco, California, is one of the most famous examples of a suspension bridge. It is one of the most flexible types of bridge design.

The suspended cables provide some flexibility for the roadway. Roadways may be less likely to break or snap during a light earthquake. However, the flexibility can also be a disadvantage. Too much shaking or high winds can make the roadway flex or even break.

Cable-Stayed Bridge

Long cables that attach from a tower to the roadway secure cable-stayed bridges. A cable-stayed bridge may look somewhat like a suspension bridge, but the connections and supports are different. The cables connect directly from the tower to the roadway. Only one tower is needed to connect the cables. The cables are rigid and extend out in a pattern from the tower to the roadway.

Cable-stayed bridges are a popular design among today's bridge engineers. The cables provide strong support and allow for interesting designs. For a very long bridge, multiple towers can be used along the roadway.

Cantilever Bridge

A cantilever bridge is one that uses horizontal structures that are supported on only one end. This type of bridge is useful for expanding the span between towers. This is especially useful for bridges that must have traffic run underneath them. There is more room for traffic underneath the bridge.

It is helpful to think of a cantilever somewhat like a diving board. The board is securely attached at one end so that the other end can hold a lot of weight. A cantilever can be attached at both ends to provide an extra-long roadway.

Bridge Failures and Lessons

When we look at today's engineering feats, we can't help but marvel at how far people have come in designing bridges. But the successes have come after some failures. Engineers and scientists follow a procedure called the engineering and design process. The process is a series of steps that helps them solve a problem.

For example, one problem might be the need to move heavy traffic in each direction over a busy port. Tall boats would have to be able to pass safely underneath the bridge. Engineers use the design process to think about the problem and possible solutions. They research the problem and look at other bridges that have been built for similar situations. They think about the advantages and disadvantages of those bridges.

Then they brainstorm solutions. They think about the materials that would be best for the project and the exact measurements needed for the height and width of the bridge. The engineers would need to know the total weight of the maximum number of cars that could pass over the bridge at the same time.

Instead of building the bridge in the hopes that their plan works, they build prototypes, or models, to test their plan. If the plan does

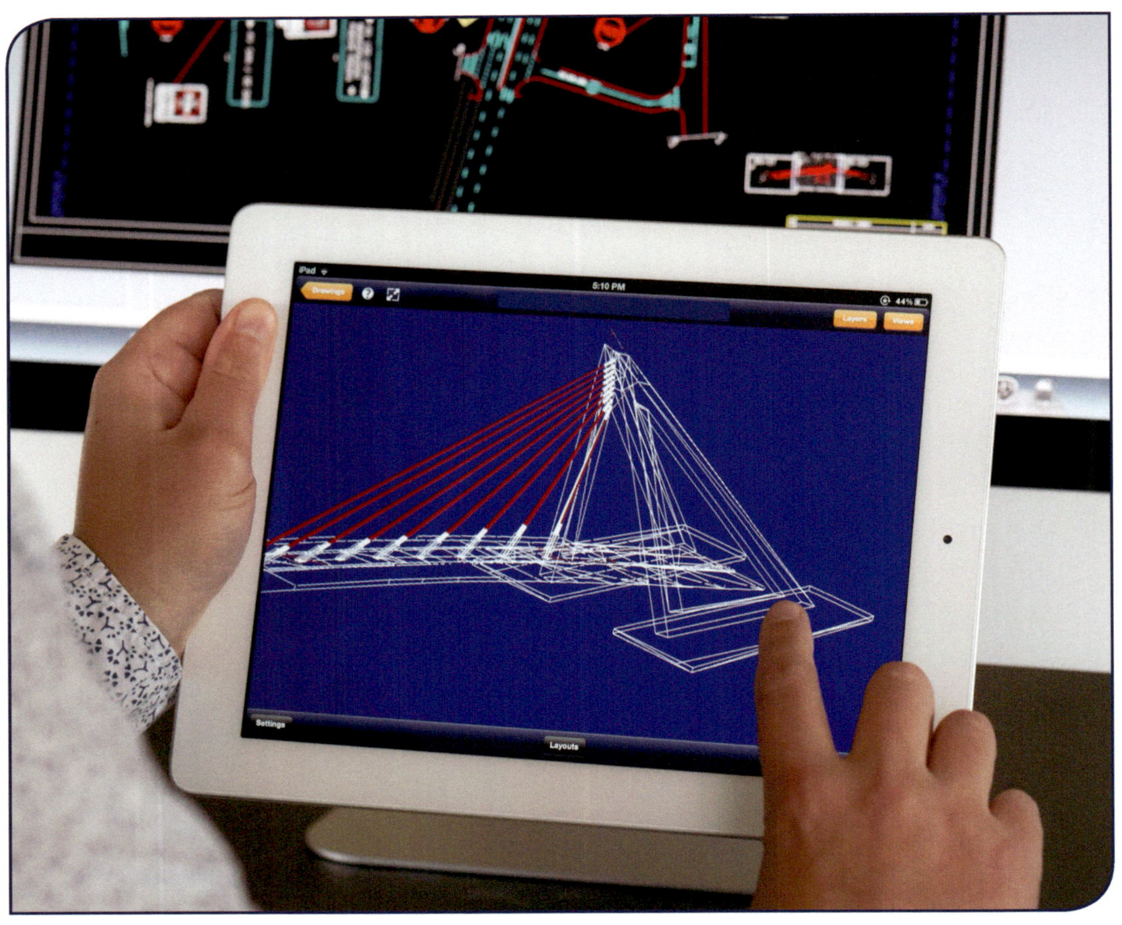

Computer Aided Design (CAD) programs help engineers plan bridges by making detailed 3D diagrams. The designs are an important part of the planning process for all architects and engineers.

not work, they can rework different parts of the solution. Testing and redesigning new ideas is one of the most important parts of the process.

The steps of the process can be followed in a different order, but they are roughly the same each time. The process helps all engineers focus on the problem and think about a good solution.

Even following all of the steps of the engineering design process, engineers make mistakes. They learn from real life use of bridges over time. Learning from mistakes is an important part of making better bridges over time.

Tacoma Narrows Bridge

One of the best-known bridge failures happened in Washington State in November 1940, just a few months after the bridge opened to the public. The Tacoma Narrows Bridge was the third-longest bridge in the world when it was built. The suspension bridge crossed over the Puget Sound. It cut the drive from Tacoma, Washington, to the Kitsap Peninsula from two and a half hours to just eleven minutes.

The suspension bridge was designed to sway a little in high winds. This would reduce strain that could cause the roadway to crack. However, the bridge moved much more than intended. As a result of the design flaw, the bridge became known as Galloping Gertie. That nickname was a play on the word "girder." A girder is a large beam of steel or iron used for constructing.

On November 7, 1940, high winds began in the early morning. This caused the deck of the bridge to bounce and sway more than it ever had before. The steel and concrete waved, bounced, and eventually began to twist as the winds increased. The roadway was quickly closed to traffic as the problem became worse. Finally, at about 10:30 am, a section of the bridge's roadway dropped into the water. This was only the beginning. Soon, the entire bridge collapsed

The Tacoma Narrows Bridge collapsed into Washington State's Puget Sound in 1940, just months after it was opened to the public. The suspension bridge twisted too much in high winds, due to poor planning and construction.

and fell into Puget Sound. Because the traffic had been stopped, no people were injured in the incident. This accident taught engineers the great responsibility of building structures for the public.

Broughton Suspension Bridge

Another important lesson in bridge building is learning the effects that different forces have on bridges. In 1831, soldiers marched across a bridge in England called the Broughton Suspension Bridge. The in-step marching of the soldiers created vibrations at the same frequency as the bridge's natural vibrations. This amplified the vibrations to a strength that the bridge could not handle. As a result, the bridge quickly weakened and broke apart.

Not only did the incident teach bridge builders about amplified vibrations, it also taught militaries to avoid such problems in the future. Since the bridge collapse in England, militaries no longer have soldiers march "in-step" as they cross bridges.

The television show *MythBusters* set out to see if it could re-create the collapse of a bridge due to repeated vibrations. After failing to break apart their model bridge, they concluded that the Broughton Suspension Bridge might have been in poor condition before the soldiers crossed it. They suspected that the extra force on the bridge weakened it further and made it collapse.

Silver Bridge

In 1967, a bridge in Point Pleasant, West Virginia, suffered a fatal collapse. This suspension bridge over the Ohio River collapsed due to corrosion on its metal chains. The collapse caused thirty-seven cars to fall into the Ohio River, killing forty-six people. The steel bridge had opened to the public in 1928, and the years of rusting affected the structure to the point of collapse.

The Silver Bridge collapse in 1967 occurred due to poor maintenance on the thirty-nine-year-old structure. The 1,756-foot bridge connected Point Pleasant, West Virginia and Gallipolis, Ohio.

The bridge was replaced by the Silver Memorial Bridge, which is a cantilever bridge that can allow ships to pass through the center of the structure when the cantilevers rise. The Silver Memorial Bridge was built about a mile downstream the Ohio River from the original Silver Bridge.

San Francisco-Oakland Bay Bridge

Sometimes even the best bridges can suffer damage from the activities of nature. The San Francisco-Oakland Bay Bridge collapsed due to a 1989 earthquake in San Francisco. The earthquake struck the city just minutes before the start of the third game of the World Series, which was being played in the city.

The vibrations of the earthquake caused the upper deck of the double-decker bridge to collapse. The bridge went through long repairs to get up and running again.

London Millennium Footbridge

When London's Millennium Footbridge opened in 2000, a big celebration was planned. Crowds gathered for the opening of this new feat of architecture. The steel suspension bridge crossed the city's River Thames. However, the weight of the crowds made the bridge vibrate slightly and in turn caused people to naturally step in time with the vibrations. This amplified the natural vibrations, similar to the problem that occurred when soldiers crossed the Broughton Suspension Bridge in 1831, causing it to collapse. The Millennium Bridge did not fall, but engineers closed the bridge for nearly two years to reinforce it and fix design problems.

Earthquakes are a major issue for bridges and a great challenge to engineers. The movement of Earth's crust shakes the foundation upon which bridges are sitting. A stable bridge must be placed on stable ground. When an area is prone to earthquakes, engineers must use advanced design methods when planning a bridge there. In 2009, the Bay Bridge was closed briefly so engineers could replace a section to make it safer in earthquakes. As technologies improve, scientists and engineers can build structures that can withstand greater stresses.

Engineering in the 21st Century

Bridge designers go through a lot of formal training to become civil engineers. Not only do they need a college degree, they also need advanced degrees and special licenses to operate in a certain state or location. Engineering uses a lot of math and science. Engineers also need to focus on the land and how it may change over time. Climate issues, possible earthquake activity, and other factors affect the designs that engineers come up with.

Engineers study thermodynamics. This branch of science is related to heat and other forms of energy. The temperatures of the places where bridges are built influence the materials engineers choose for their projects. For example, a bridge in Florida will face different temperature changes than a bridge in Alaska. The types of steel, the connections between joints, and the length of time that materials last are all important factors in planning for a strong bridge that will last well into the future.

Now more than ever, engineers must build with the future in mind. The changing climate affects Earth's structure. Nature has an impact on the human-made structures we plan. And a concern for rising populations and strained resources makes planning even more important. Here are some of the biggest concerns that bridge builders face in the twenty-first century.

Earthquake Zones

Earthquakes occur most often in areas where plates of Earth's crust meet. California is one of these areas. Places that are more likely to get earthquakes must have the strongest bridges and structures. They should be able to withstand more shaking and movement than structures in areas that are not where Earth's crust meets.

Remember that bridges connect two areas of land. If a bridge is destroyed during an earthquake, the areas are no longer connected. People can be in danger if they are isolated.

The best thing engineers can do in areas prone to earthquakes is to plan ahead. They use reinforced materials that can withstand strong shaking. This cuts down on repairs they might need to do after a quake. It could even save the entire structure from falling.

After the 1989 San Francisco earthquake damaged the eastern span of the San Francisco-Oakland Bay Bridge, engineers looked at the bridge more closely. They decided that the eastern span of the bridge needed to be replaced. The new bridge section would be expensive, but it needed to be safe.

Based on earthquake prediction data, scientists and engineers assumed the bridge would likely be hit with an earthquake during its expected lifespan. This is about 150 years. That meant that they would have to make sure the bridge would be able to withstand a future earthquake.

The suspension cables on the new span are reinforced. Hundreds of wire cables are bundled together to make a larger cable. And then several of those bundled cables are bunched together into one strong steel cable that can withstand great amounts of movement and jostling during a quake.

On October 17, 1989, an earthquake collapsed a section of the San Francisco-Oakland Bay Bridge. Forty-two people were killed in the incident, and plans for a safer replacement bridge began.

By the time it was finally finished in 2013, the more earthquake-proof eastern span of the San Francisco-Oakland Bay Bridge cost more than $6 billion to build.

The base of the bridge is strong concrete and steel, anchored to the rock under the bay. Heavy concrete spikes, or posts, called pilings extend almost 200 feet (60 m) into the bedrock under the bay. This gives extra support to the sections of bridge attached above it. In the event of a sudden or violent movement of the ground, the reinforced base of the bridge can help protect the entire structure.

Engineering decisions like the ones made on the San Francisco-Oakland Bay Bridge are very expensive. The rebuilding of the damaged section of the bridge cost $6.5 billion. The cost of protecting the public is an even greater consideration for civil engineers and bridge builders. When building for the future, cost and safety are a top priority for engineers.

Environmental Concerns

Climate is the weather conditions a place experiences over a long period of time. Climate scientists have recorded evidence of climate changes that could affect the way we live in the near future. The climate conditions are predicted to bring more severe weather and temperatures in the future. This means that the structures we build now and into the future must be able to withstand these severe changes.

An increase in hurricane or tornado activity, for example, requires that engineers build bridges that are stronger than ever. Flooding is also an important issue. Many bridges are built to be high enough for ships to travel underneath them. Future flooding would change the height that a bridge should be to allow ship traffic underneath. Engineers rely on precise calculations so the structure they are building

Out with the Old

How can engineers update bridges to make them safer, more modern, and ready to last through the next century? Many bridges have thousands of cars crossing them every day. There will be major traffic problems if the bridges are shut down and removed to make way for new ones. That's why engineers often work on building a new bridge right beside the old bridge. While the new bridge is being built, traffic continues to flow on the old bridge. When the new bridge is finished, it is open to the public. Then the old bridge is torn down. The process allows for a continuation of traffic and safety of the community.

Replacing the Tappan Zee Bridge in New York City took nearly five years. The Mario M. Cuomo Bridge was constructed directly next to the old Tappan Zee Bridge to allow traffic to continue as normal.

fits within the environment. If the environment changes, engineers must be ready to problem solve and make public structures safe.

Sustainable Materials

The environment is a big concern for engineers not only because of climate issues, but also because of available resources. The things we use around us in our environment are called resources. Wood is a resource from trees. Steel is a resource from iron. Many resources are limited on Earth. Once humans use them up, it takes a long time for them to form by Earth's natural processes.

Making steel is a process that can pollute the environment, too. Any factory process can create pollution over time. That's why it is important to think about the materials used to build bridges. Finding a material that is long lasting and easy to produce will make the best bridges.

Steel is durable and strong and is used on most modern bridges. Steel lasts about 100 years, so a steel bridge built today may last well into the twenty-second century. The best way to make a design that is sustainable and environmentally responsible is to make the construction as lightweight as possible. Lightweight materials are less damaging to the environment because less energy is used to create the materials. The process of making a set amount of lightweight steel does not pollute the air or water as much as the process of making a heavier volume of the same amount of steel.

So, when engineers think about the future of bridge building, it is important to think about the materials that will be used.

Cars, Cars Everywhere

When cars first appeared on roads in the early 1900s, there was not as much worry about the weight of the traffic going over bridges. There were no standstills for hours on the roadways in rush-hour traffic. Some of the bridges were left over from days when horses traveled across them. When steel became easy to produce, more bridges were built. But cars were not as common, and traffic was not what it is today.

According to an article in *Automotive News*, there are millions of cars on the road in the United States today. By 2021, that number is expected to be about twenty million. Roads, highways, and bridges

The weight of heavy traffic on bridge roadways has become an engineering challenge. Bridges in the future must account for predicted increases in traffic, and some of today's older bridges may need reinforcement.

connect every location. This means that bridges can face the strain of extra loads on the decks. If fifty cars cross a bridge roadway in a half hour, the bridge does not face the total load of those fifty cars all at once. But if the fifty cars are stuck on the roadway in a traffic jam, the bridge must be strong enough to bear the total weight of all fifty cars at once. That's why bridge building in the future must use all of the technology possible to make strong structures that can withstand heavy loads.

Cost

When we look at some of the most breathtaking bridges in the world, we may not think about the price tag. But cost is a major factor for engineers who must plan the cost of the production. They must consider the cost of everything, from the last foot of steel to the last bolt used to secure the roadway. Even the cost of delivery of materials and preparing the land costs money. Budgets can be strict for engineering firms or even government projects that pay for building bridges.

Just fixing damage to bridges because of storms or high winds can cost in the millions of dollars. Making bridges from the first designs through the opening of the structure can easily run into the billons of dollars.

Engineers are always experimenting with new ideas for how to make bridges using materials that are better and last longer. Even though bridges cost a lot to build, that cost is considered to be less if the bridge will stand and need little repair over a long period of time. Regular maintenance and upkeep on bridges can be costly, so the materials used can be important.

The materials, the location, and environmental factors all contribute to the final cost of the bridge. Engineers must consider each of these factors before making a final decision. Inventing new, stronger, longer-lasting materials can help make bridge building more cost effective in the future.

Bridges of Tomorrow

The basic bridge types explained in chapter 1 have stood the test of time. Many steel bridges are able to last for a century before they have to be replaced. Basic repairs along the way can keep bridges safe for the public. The basic beam, suspension, cable-stayed, and other bridge designs work well. Engineers will continue to use those into the future. But they are also experimenting with new ideas to support more traffic on modern roadways. They consider temperature changes, land features, and any other features that might affect how long the structure can last.

Some of the engineering marvels of the twenty-first century include bridges that are longer and taller than ever before. These high-tech bridges can do more than just resist earthquakes and high winds. Some of them are amazing to look at because of their inventive designs. Others are impressive because of where they go and the areas of land they connect.

When looking for the most impressive bridges of the twenty-first century, look to developing countries. The United States had some of the most impressive bridges of the twentieth century. They represented growth and innovation at the time. Now, some of those earlier bridges are old and decaying. They are going through repairs. Some are being replaced.

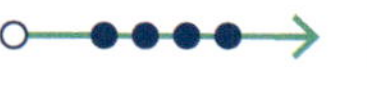

Becoming a Bridge Builder

There are many people who work on different stages of bridge building. The first people involved survey the land and find the location to build. Then crews are needed to clear the land and make it ready for building. Construction crews may work nonstop for years to make a structure as large as a bridge. They work under the guidance of engineers and construction leaders who check their work. The work does not stop after the bridge is open to the public. Bridges need to be constantly inspected to make sure they are safe. Repair crews may work on repairs while the bridge is open to the public.

However, in some areas of the world, highways and ports are being built for the first time. Areas in China, India, and Africa, for example, did not have growth in industry at the same time the United States did. Many of their roads, highways, ports, and harbors are still being built. Bridges are needed to connect these new structures. These parts of the world have some of the most impressive new bridges in the world. They are architectural marvels, and they also function well for the high volume traffic of cars and ships.

Here are some of the most impressive modern bridges built in the twenty-first century that will inspire future bridge builders.

Magdeburg Water Bridge

This German structure is the longest aqueduct for water traffic in the world. The Magdeburg Water Bridge opened in 2003. It allows ships to cross *above* the Elbe River. This is an impressive feat. Before the bridge was built, ships had trouble going from one area of elevation to another in the region. They had to take a detour of 7.5 miles

The 918-meter (3,012-foot) Magdeburg Water Bridge in Germany allows boats to travel over the Elbe River, an amazing accomplishment in engineering.

(12 kilometers) to get to a structure that would lift the boats to a higher elevation so they could continue their journey. The new aqueduct saves ships time and connects Berlin's network of harbors with ports along the Rhine River.

When building bridges for the future, engineers consider the trade in a region. Shipping has always been an important way to get goods from one place to another. If improved engineering can make shipping easier and faster with bridges, then shipping can be improved in the future.

Danyang-Kunshan Grand Bridge

China has been experiencing industrial growth since the early 2000s. This boom in building and manufacturing of goods created a new demand for faster transportation. There are many mountainous areas in China. Roads and bridges had never connected these areas well for business. Hundreds of new bridges had to be built to mountain areas. These new bridges are modern, using state-of-the-art materials and designs. As a result, some are record-setters.

The Danyang-Kunshan Grand Bridge in China is currently the longest railroad bridge in the world. At 102.4 miles (164.8 km), the bridge connects complex land features such as rivers, lakes, canals, rice paddies in low areas, and areas of land that are very uneven. When the bridge opened in 2011, it broke the record for the longest bridge, formerly held by a bridge in Louisiana.

Another impressive part of the bridge is the protective section that goes above it. The section was built on two thousand pillars that provide extra strength. There are also 450,000 tons (408,233 metric tons) of steel that make up reinforced cables. This extra protection makes the bridge able to withstand typhoons, which are common in the area. It can also stand up to some of the strongest earthquakes

The Danyang-Kunshan Grand Bridge is located near Shanghai, China. It took five years to build, and at 102.4 miles it's currently the longest railroad bridge in the world.

and even the direct hit of ships that weigh up to 300,000 tons (272,155 metric tons).

In the future, more bridges will be able to use the design features of the Danyang-Kunshan Grand Bridge. Building over difficult terrain in areas with extreme weather will be important for the safety of the population.

Out of this World Design

Some bridges make us think of the future just by looking at them. Some look like futuristic structures out of science fiction movies.

Seri Wawasan Bridge

One example is the Seri Wawasan Bridge in Malaysia. The cable-stayed bridge connects an area of the capital city Putrajaya with a nearby island.

The cables of the cable-stayed bridge connect to one supporting post at one end of the structure. The connections along the post make

The Seri Wawasan Bridge in Putrajaya, Malaysia, has a modern design that looks like the strings of a harp. It was opened to the public in 2003.

the cables look like they are twisted and curved when viewed from the roadway. The bridge opened in 2003 and has three wide lanes and a shoulder for emergency vehicles. First responders sometimes have trouble getting cars on and off bridge roadways when there is an accident. It can be especially dangerous to access accidents when bridges are over water. Providing extra room for these emergencies is important, especially when the bridges are in busy cities with a lot of traffic.

Helix Bridge

Pedestrian bridges have the ability to be even more spectacular than bridges for trains or cars. That's because they don't have to be as long or hold as heavy a load. Engineers built a structure called the Helix Bridge across the Singapore River to connect two areas of the city that go around a marina.

The unique thing about this curved bridge is that it mimics the shape of a double helix. The double helix is the structure of the human DNA molecule. The structure of the bridge makes sightseeing easy and can even provide shade for pedestrians because of the way it is covered on the top.

The arc surrounding the entire bridge gives the feel that the pedestrians are walking through the helix. The LED lighting on the bridge makes it spectacular at night. It is just as much an amusement for the people at the marina looking at it as for the people walking through it.

The Helix Bridge is an example of the creativity that civil engineers can have when they build bridges and other structures for the public.

Bridge Made of Recycled Materials

With our concerns today about abusing resources, builders and engineers try to consider the environment when they design. In 2011, a 90-foot-long (27 m) bridge in Scotland was opened to the public. It

The Helix Bridge is a pedestrian walkway that connects two sections of a marina in Singapore.

was made from more than 50 tons (45 metric tons) of recycled plastic. The bridge covers the River Tweed in Scotland. It can carry a load of up to 44 tons (40 metric tons). Recycled materials are not as strong as steel, but using them has benefits. Recycled materials do not require maintenance and do not rot or become damaged by pests like wood does. The bridge is also recyclable, so it will not be wasted when it becomes old. The parts can be recycled and used again.

A bridge made from recycled materials can save resources. Looking into the twenty-first century, this will be increasingly important. With greater populations using more resources and energy, it will be important to come up with alternatives to using new resources.

One of the most important things about building bridges throughout the twenty-first century is to consider the environment. The more the environment changes, the better our plans for engineering will have to be so we can have safe and strong structures to last into the future.

1st century CE

Romans build aqueducts for moving water.

1345

Ponte Vecchio Bridge in Florence, Italy, is built. It is still in use today.

15th century

Earliest known suspension bridge is built.

1779

The Iron Bridge in Shropshire, England, is built. It was the first iron bridge, with a single span of about 100 feet (30 m).

1883

The Brooklyn Bridge opens.

1937

The Golden Gate Bridge opens.

1940

The Tacoma Narrows Bridge collapses.

2003

The Magdeburg Water Bridge opens in Germany.

2010

Seri Wawasan Bridge opens in Malaysia.

2011

Danyang-Kunshan Grand Bridge opens in China.

History.com. "1989 San Francisco Earthquake." Retrieved September 3, 2017. http://www.history.com/topics/1989-san-francisco-earthquake.

History of Bridges. "Truss Bridge—Types, History, Facts and Design." Retrieved September 8, 2017. http://www.historyofbridges.com/facts-about-bridges.

Howell, Elizabeth. "Why Do Soldiers Break Stride on a Bridge?" *Live Science*, May 22, 2013. https://www.livescience.com/34608-break-stride-frequency-of-vibration.html.

Interesting Engineering. "Roman Arch Bridges: How Much Weight Can They Hold?" Retrieved September 3, 2017. https://interestingengineering.com/roman-arch-bridges-weight-hold.

Kim, Sun. "Europe's First Bridge Made from Recycled Plastic." *ZDNet*, October 31, 2011. http://www.zdnet.com/article/europes-first-bridge-made-from-recycled-plastic.

Lamb, Robert, and Michael Morrissey. "How Bridges Work." *How Stuff Works*. Retrieved September 3, 2017. http://science.howstuffworks.com/engineering/civil/bridge7.htm.

Pasternack, Alex. "The Strangest, Most Spectacular Bridge Collapse (and How We Got It Wrong)." *Motherboard*, December 14, 2015. https://motherboard.vice.com/en_us/article/kb78w3/the-myth-of-galloping-gertie.

Science Buddies. "Engineering and Design Process." Retrieved September 3, 2017. https://www.sciencebuddies.org/science-fair-projects/engineering-design-process/engineering-design-process-steps.

Sperling, Daniel, and Deborah Gordon. "Two Billion Cars: Transforming a Culture." *TR News*, November/December 2008. http://onlinepubs.trb.org/onlinepubs/trnews/trnews259 billioncars.pdf.

Study.com. "Civil Engineering: Requirements for Becoming a Civil Engineer." Retrieved September 8, 2017. http://study.com/articles/Civil_Engineering_Requirements_for_Becoming_a_Civil_Engineer.html.

West Virginia Department of Transportation. "Silver Bridge." Retrieved September 8, 2017. http://www.transportation.wv.gov/highways/bridge_facts/Modern-Bridges/Pages/Silver.aspx.

Wta, Alex. "Seri Wawasan Bridge–Putrajaya, Malaysia." *World Travel Attractions*. Retrieved September 3, 2017. http://www.worldtravelattractions.com/sri-wawasan-bridge-putrajaya-malaysia.

abutment The support at the end of a bridge to hold the force of a load on top of the bridge.

aqueduct A channel for moving water, usually on a bridge.

cable-stayed A bridge type that is supported by cables connecting the roadway to tall posts.

caisson A large, watertight chamber that keeps water out so construction workers can work underwater.

cantilever A bridge type that has a long beam attached just on one end.

climate The weather conditions for an area over a period of time.

corrosion Decay.

engineering-design process The steps followed by engineers to explore and test new ideas.

girder A large beam of iron or steel used for bridge building.

load The amount of weight or mass pushing against something.

piling Heavy post or stake that supports a large structure.

prototype A model.

sustainable Able to be maintained for a long time.

thermodynamics The branch of science that has to do with heat and energy.

truss A type of bridge with a supportive framework, usually in repeating triangular shapes.

vibration Repeating movements.

Books

Hardyman, Robyn. *Bridges*. New York, NY: Powerkids Press, 2017.

Hoena, Blake. *Building the Golden Gate Bridge*. Mankato, MN: Capstone Press, 2014.

Squire, Ann. *Extreme Bridges*. New York, NY: Children's Press, 2015.

Stine, Megan. *Where Is the Brooklyn Bridge?* New York, NY: Penguin Workshop, 2016.

Websites

Building Big: Bridges

www.pbs.org/wgbh/buildingbig/bridge

The website provides links to information about famous bridges around the world and links to information about bridge-building projects for kids and other bridge resources.

Easy Science for Kids

www.easyscienceforkids.com/all-about-bridges

The website gives information about all kinds of bridges and includes fun facts about bridges

PBS Learning Media

https://ny.pbslearningmedia.org/collection/structures

The website provides links to bridge-related projects for children, including miniature bridge-building challenges and other bridge-related design challenges.

INDEX